LOVE LOVE, LIKE NO ONE ELSE

LRC

GOOD DIE YOUNG

2

CONTENTS

Me

cigarettes

who named you, cigarettes, i wonder?
oh, heartbreaking secrets you keep under.
they named you cigarettes, no wonder.

you burn the secrets told, my dear,
unlike the cold-blooded ones present here.
if only i thought they were right,
would you ever have crossed my sight?

as the number shoots up, my death is near,
unlike the filthy humans, i presume no fear.
with silence, kill me, not words like her.
name the day, make me disappear.

oh, was it too hard to get it in?
it's not the world which is cruel, but the people you
let in.

days with love have gone so far,

for nations, titles, and men so brave.

love, could i ask for someone

crying beside my grave?

if i die before i reach your arms,

will you still tell, how much you loved me-

to the moon?

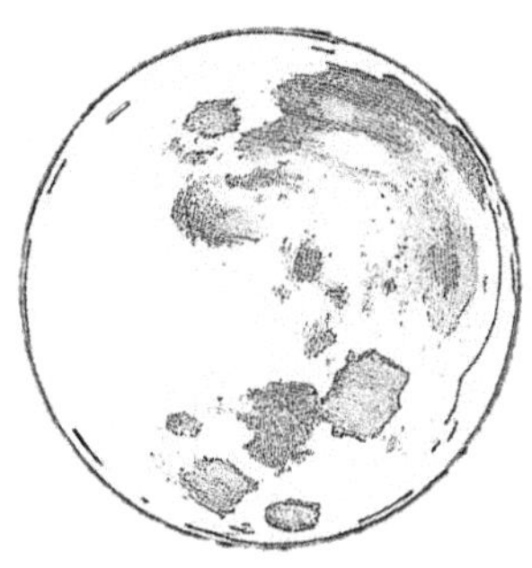

could i wish for something?

not so big to call me greedy,

not so small to call me dumb.

not too much to call it a party,

not too less to call me numb.

could i wish for something

to make sure i'm human?

feed a flower to my grave,

not too many to call it a burden.

from sleepless nights
to sleepless nights-
love

life did want to teach me something,
too young that i did know nothing.

monsters screaming inside my head,
fighting demons, being dead.

matured young,
feelings swung.
someone get it off my head.

the day i set foot out of my grave,

the day my promise-my promise-was saved.

if pain meant peace and has to be,

you are not somewhere you have to be.

"promises are not hard

to keep afterall."

the one who wants everything fights with
the one who has got everything, but not for
what he wants.

i only consider someone my enemy
if they are equally strong as me.
funny how someone of my caliber
won't consider anyone enemies.

sometimes you really want it,

sometimes you want others to see you've

got it.

anyone can be what you want to be,

but not everyone can be who you want

to be.

when it comes to love,
every head shall bow,
everyone shall see,
every mouth shall confess,
every heart shall beat.

say,
he was the weakest receiver but the greatest
lover.

love, the devil felt when dim,

was an angel's pity on him.

i shall make her name reach heaven, with
my roots ruling hell.

i have her photos
a lot of them
made sapphires and rubies worthless gems

i have her memories
with me inside,
days like them
when we laughed and cried

i have a request
made it a promise
cost it my life, i shall show the world
who a gentleman is.

the time i've burnt,
to the friends i've earned,

opinions shared,
emotions cared,

tears hidden,
feelings forbidden.

one day i shall,
one day i will,

shout it out loud:
"i have made my parents proud."

he was never loved.

with her, he was comforting her with the words he
wished to hear.

say my name,

say it loud,

let the world know how it sounds.

who am i?

from downtown,

let them know who owns the crown.

say her name,

let them speak,

about the king

who bows to his queen.

where do i go,

if your voice won't let me sleep?

where do i go,

with you inside of me?

where do i go,

do i have nowhere else to flee?

where do i go,

if your love is all i need?

even if we couldn't stay together,

and destiny falls apart,

i just want to hear you say,

"he really loved me with all that he got."

i want to fall in love with you
every single day like it's the first day
spend the time like it waits for us
and end the night like the night we met.

in the middle of a chaos

it struck me

27

"should i fight for what i've lost or move on with
what i've got?"

the worst of me met the best of her.

the best of me will make the worst of her the

best of her so the best of her can be the

rest of her.

i was in love with her and,
i wanted to be loved-
you shouldn't expect anything in love-
so i wasn't loved.

some kind words to keep me going
"how are you doing?"

is it a sin to be loved?
is it a sin to expect 'love' in love?

no one to call
no one to text
no one at all
just me
smoking cigarettes

lighting it up,
one by one
fighting my thoughts
all at once.

time goes by

time flies

warriors in history carved in sculptures

good to bad eaten by vultures

time goes by

time flies

for, everything known to mankind failed

to survive

he held his love close to his heart.

love is war
wrong or right
people who asked for
got hurt inside

be it the angel or the devil
once they're hurt
they'll change their will

neither the angel
nor the devil
got my promises to fulfill

who was i before you?

someone with no emotions but values

who was i before you?

someone who throned his ego, a crown

who was i before you?

someone whom i barely recognize now.

i wasn't expecting it to come
i never expected it to leave

the closer she gets, the deeper it sounds

the sadder it gets, the beautiful it becomes.

35

lips missed
eyes kissed

heart mumbled
fear trembled

felt it all in
i let it fade

what's the point
when i've lost all faith.

hundred lines to make her mine

hundred lies she left behind

if you blame it, you never earned it
if you never felt it, you never meant it.

good times is all i asked for,
i've got people praying for my fall
mistakes broke me harder than i thought
i carry no regrets, not at all.

if meant to be fails to be

a part of me will lose the most of me.

"i will search for you
in my last smile"

loved enough to be forever missed

broken to become an artist, worthy.

42

'

a florist never receives a flower
for himself.

43

loving pain, hurts a few men
let it hurt, it keeps me human.

it is important to sound alive than to
sound right.

45

its not the dream we are living in

it's the reality i made that made you

feel like one

if the pain hurts no more,

who am i battling myself for?

47

people call your necessities as needs
and desires as greed.
how is it greed when my desire
is everything i need.

i've hated love more
than i've loved hate.

is it a part of life or is it

the part that costs my life?

mechanical body

mechanical body filled with meat
impossible to escape until defeat

what is this tingly feel in my tummy?
overflowing emotions from me

i never asked for it but it feels nice
out of my control, walking on thin ice

i feel important for the first time
is this the part of being a machine?
happiness feels like a crime
struck by a lightning
that's what i mean.

bloody hands create beautiful poems.

52

she crossed the path of my life,

i remembered her for the rest of my life.

53

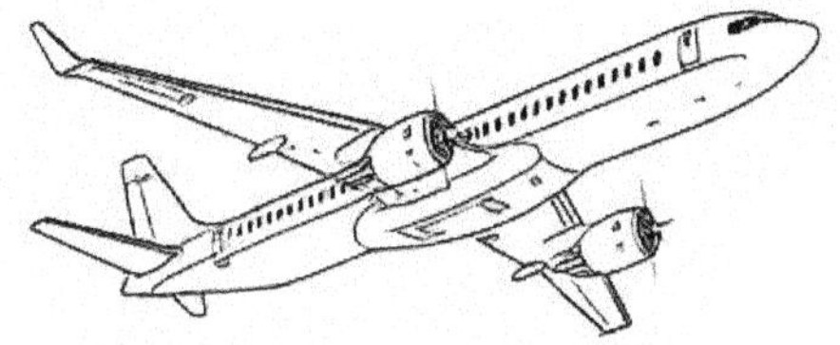

a curse followed

for a thousand years

54

the cursed one's fall hard for the one's meant

to break the curse.

i missed a little of me
who i used to be
before we called it
our destiny.

love is beautiful because

everyone has their own understanding

love hurts because

everyone has their own understanding.

they said:

"she was a chapter not your love,
but she was a chapter you loved."

in the eyes of love

there are no wrong ones.

it's time to sleep
i closed my eyes
is that how things end?
its's no surprise

am i luckiest to be the unluckiest?

am i unluckiest to be the luckiest?

my tears dried
it's time to sleep
at least to close my eyes
knowing it's hard for me

if that's how things end
I would say my goodbye
waiting for all your lies
to just be lies.

baby maybe it was never all of me

big time sucker for this destiny

baby maybe love was never meant for me

heartfelt curse worth memories

if all those stars could look at me

the way we make our memories

they would be burning their life to jealousy

because they are not me

for once, i want to be on the

other side of the pen.

You

your warmth is all i need

your breath enough to breathe

last words of mine spoke goodbye

there i hid my promise, no lie

bangles

whispered under her breath,
"could you get me bangles?"
between living and dying, watched
my tiny soul tangle
blushed and rushed, i shall get it this time,
ordinarily beautiful to make it divine

walked so far,
till my legs gave out,
my eyes willed strong
to see them be yours.

jealousy filled me as they wrapped
around your arms
soon did i wonder, i wasn't at fault

seemed like the lost river who reached her
mother fall,
graceful to see things from where they
actually are.

the things which happen without any

meanings are the meaningful ones.

you saw the journey of us

which i didn't see

you want me to be better

and i will be.

if not for your eyes

what would i be looking at?

if not your smile

what would i be falling for?

if not you then,

who would i consider worth dying for?

if destiny does not make it happen

i shall rewrite it.

when you see me

like a stranger

i hate it, i hate it

when you want to

talk to me

just say it, i want it

when you care for

somebody

even if it's not me

it's okay, i envy

it's everyone except me

why me?

why not me?

is there a heart i can borrow?

only to love it like there's no tomorrow

for all these days you've faced 'em sorrows

there's only love left from tomorrow.

for the first time, i noticed her eyes

not the colour

not the shine

but looking at mine

star gazing

cold winter night, i was looking at the stars,
little did i know, we'd get this far.
stars cleared darkness with light,
one such star crossed my sight.

wild winter winds freezing everywhere,
got her by my side, i've got love wear
holding her hands, miles together
hours felt like minutes, with her forever

you'd be looking at my star,
for whom i came all the way so far
end my life when i rise and shine,
not this beautiful moment of mine.

"lets go stargazing someday."
to all the beautiful things,
people think end up in heaven,

she's someone my poems got

but the heavens, not.

fame?

what is fame when its money?

money?

what is money when its health?

health?

what is health in front of time?

time?

what is time in front of the girl who froze

mine.

people don't change
when you cry,
feelings don't fade
when tears dry.

love? hate? personality twist?

hateful reasons gently kissed.

name the reason, line or gist,

how many goodnights have i missed?

older the love, deeper it gets

sooner the end, less beautiful it is.

81

no matter how long love takes you,

you are always closer to the last line

than the first time.

the war grew

within the lines she drew.

words which matter

lost its value.

don't cry if you lose,

when the fight is done.

the fight might be over,

but the war has just begun.

for she's a poem,

her name be my favorite line,

her voice be my favorite rhyme.

someday

we walk the same path,
yet miles apart

we see the same thing,
yet we disagree

time plays,
we part ways

but someday, if our paths cross
i will hold your hands and
make sure you're never lost.

when you told me it didn't matter,

your tears told how deep you were

shattered.

writing a few sad lines at the end

of a love story does not make the

love look bad,

it makes the story

look beautiful.

bruises and scars don't matter to me,

feelings deeper than the dead wild sea

lies over lies to set me free-

how beautiful can you be?

i've got a lot that i never wanted,

i've lost a lot that i always wanted.

how far would i go for her?
she asked.

far enough to get lost and wonder-
wonder to wander to wonder
i shall hold my promise and your name,
walk in straight, knocking on heaven's gate.
for if the heavens denied your name,
i shall make them sing your fairy tale.

but she never asked.

tears ran out

stopped right up

before it could fall

it had its time

thinking about you

if you were mine

its not love which hurts,

it's the dream you dreamt

of the time wanted to be spent

it would have been better if the

"would have's" had actually had.

would have never happened

if it hadn't had.

nicknames are lame,

i love calling you by your name.

94

right way, lost mine,

right person, wrong time.

love story, last line,

was love ever mine?

truths don't hurt as much as your lies.

oh darling, my dear,

the day has come, the day i fear.

it's the fairy tale's nightmare,

ending the last line, the last line here.

does it really matter how it started,

when you know how its going to end?

i wanna see you next to me,

around my arms, half asleep.

did it all happen

for it not to happen?

sometimes you got to learn to love

someone by not loving someone.

i held her face close to mine,

promising love lasting lifetime.

in the blink of an eye, everything was gone,

disappeared like they were never born.

blue wind

once blew a blue wind,
mystically passed through me,
neither the blue, the deep sea owns,
nor the blue, the diamond crowns.

lived through all four seasons,
this one's different for some reason.
darkest during the day,
shined bright throughout the night.

blue was never that beautiful,
never before, ever after.

how does it feel resting deeper

in my memories than my dreams?

i wish the moon adores you the same

way you adore it.

i'm staying

not for who you are to me,

but for who you have been to me.

we loved each other,
but not loud.

we made eye contact,
but broke it often.

we cared for each other,
but in private.

we call it not this time,
when it needs some time.

hold it tight till it fades or

set it free for whatever it takes.

-destiny

you think you're not much, but

you're the oasis in the desert,

i quenched.

how are you not special, when you're

the first person who comes to my mind

when i think about myself.

what is death

when an artist falls in love with you?

take me to your nightmares,

watch me drown your darkness.

what is destiny?

if its not you and me?

this is not a poem or a rhyme,

be honest,

are you fine?

she was there for me,

she couldn't care for me.

115

the love was untold,

when silence echoed.

is it all?

is this all you wanted to say?
is this a feeling which i defend?
is this why i lost my way?
is this how it all ends?

ending breath

with endless love,

to forever and now.

only the real flowers

shed petals.

what if you make me feel pain?

will i ever be the same?

what if we cross paths once again?

will i ever get to call you by your name?

the same way like the first day

will it ever be the same?

the first time i met you,

i immediately knew it'd be

impossible to forget you.

"i wanted to be lost when i found you,

i wanted to be lost when i lost you."

you broke your heart to lie,

how hard was it to lie and not cry?

lies that don't mean to cheat me,

lies that don't mean to taunt me,

lies that can never hurt me,

lies, all lies, let it be.

do you want to cry,

when it hurts to smile?

to see the stars you like

fade in front of your eyes

kiss my lips, not for the last time,

i'm a half dead man with a broken smile.

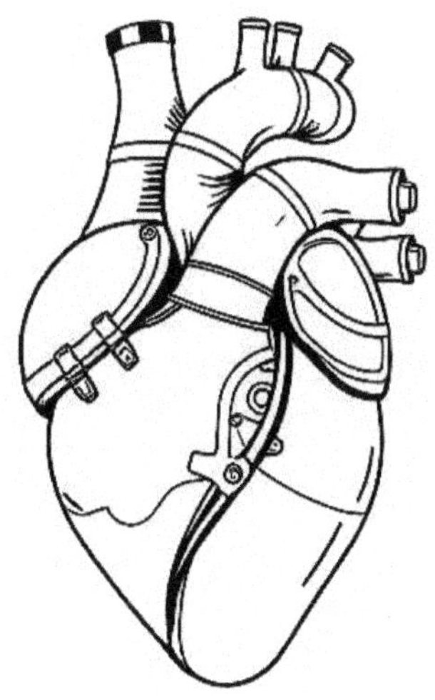

it hurts, how can i disagree?

when its you who felt it more than me.

i guess, it was all for now,

it's time to rest my pen down.

127

i'll leave the next page blank

to continue my fairytale, once you

comeback.

Known by his stage name LRC, Kartikeya LRC is a versatile artist. He is an enthusiastic songwriter, aspiring actor, and director who uses his love of movies and his ability to express himself through poetry and songwriting, among other artistic endeavors. This is his first book as a writer and poet, and he is 21 years old. LRC started his artistic career at the age of 19, and by the time he was 21, he had a better grasp of the intricacies of love. He feels that there are no wrong answers to the question, "What is love?" and that love is a very unique experience. Every individual's viewpoint is legitimate, and LRC examines the various ways that love is perceived and communicated in his work. The speaker cherishes his character and essence more than his accomplishments or activities, as seen by his favorite quote, "I want to be remembered as someone who was something, not someone who did something."

About the book :

The message of "Love love, like no one else" is to embrace love rather than offer a definition. The notion that each person's definition of love is unique and legitimate is celebrated in this book, which exhorts readers to give up trying to find the "right" definition. It provides viewpoints that shed light on the intricacies, pleasures, and tragedies of love instead.

Through provocative observations, the book serves as a reminder to live fully and completely in love, including its agony. As the writer so eloquently puts it, "love love, like no one else, more than loving a person more than anyone else."

To experience the essence of love in a way that feels exclusively your own, read this book—not to figure out what it is.

www.ingramcontent.com/pod-product-compliance
Lightning Source LLC
Chambersburg PA
CBHW041332120726

48005CB00014B/2218